CONTENTS

FOREWORD

A county with a timeless natural beauty yet which continues to change and develop with the times in which we live

Dorset's natural beauty may be timeless, but there is much about the county that has changed drastically over the years.

This book, brought to you by the Daily Echo and the Dorset Echo, presents a fascinating collection of pictures documenting some of those changes.

Some of the photographs in these pages show the county as it was when Thomas Hardy, TE Lawrence or even Robert Louis Stevenson knew it.

Others show how the arrival of the motor car, the expansion of industry or the tragedy of war have changed our towns.

Still more demonstrate how the building of roads, homes and commercial developments have transformed parts of Dorset in more recent times.

Look at the photographs of central Poole from 40 years ago and you might struggle to recognise the place.

The landmarks in old pictures of Bournemouth, Christchurch, Weymouth or Dorchester might be more familiar, but these towns have still changed dramatically.

On the other hand, some of the county's most beautiful rural spots remain essentially the same places they have been for centuries – from its picturesque inland villages to the spectacular beauty of the Jurassic Coast.

We hope you enjoy all the scenes in this book and that it will prompt some enjoyable reminiscences

about the way your own part of Dorset has changed over the decades and perhaps motivate a visit to a favourite beauty spot or two!

Thankfully, the one thing about Dorset that never changes is that it is a wonderful place to live.

Front cover: The Pier, Bournemouth, pictured in 1897 and today. *Early picture courtesy of The Francis Frith Collection*

CHRISTCHURCH

The 'place between two rivers', a tenth century Priory, a castle ruin and the creation of the Bailey Bridge

Christchurch has a history going back even further than that of its magnificent 900-year-old Priory. The town was originally the fortified Saxon burgh of Tweoxneam – later corrupted as Twynham – meaning the place between two rivers.

The Priory, built on the site of former Saxon chapels, still remains the town's most famous and striking building, although it is not the oldest – Place Mill on the Quay is mentioned in the Domesday Book and was a working building until the early 1900s.

Other notable buildings include the 17th century workhouse which has been the Red House Museum since 1951, the 14th century former Court House, and the Constable's House,

built next door to the Priory in the mid-12th century. And there are the ruins of the town's castle, also built in the 12th century.

But while the town promotes itself as the place where "time is pleasant", time has not stood still. The 1980s saw the arrival of the Saxon Square shopping centre, recently refurbished, while housing sprang up rapidly throughout much of the last century, along with commercial and shopping developments.

Fishing was for a long time a big part of Christchurch's economy, as was smuggling in centuries gone by. In the 20th century, the town became known for its aviation and defence industries, and Donald Bailey developing the Bailey Bridge

there during the Second World War. Christchurch is also home, of course, to the controversially named Bournemouth Airport. Today, tourism is vitally important to the town, which happily shares its mix of the historic and the modern with countless thousands of delighted visitors.

Christchurch High Street circa 1910, showing the tram lines that had been installed in 1905, and the street today

1910 picture courtesy of the Red House Museum

A patriotic peace parade in the High Street in 1918
Picture courtesy of Red House Museum

The Old Town Hall and Mayor's Parlour today (top centre)

The High Street in the early 1950s, showing shops along the west side, and the town library. *Picture courtesy of Red House Museum*

The same scene today (bottom centre)

The Bargates area in Christchurch in 1982, before it was extensively redeveloped (main image)

The scene today, with modern shops and office buildings (above)

A quieter High Street in 1961, and in 2014
Picture courtesy of Red House Museum

The original unblended images (above)

Mudeford pictured in 1948, before its promenade was built (left)

The same spot today, with visitors crab fishing off the prom (above)

Christchurch and its Priory, viewed from the air in 1954 (below)

Mudeford Quay seen from above circa 1960 (opposite)

Bridge Street under flood water in
the 1950s and in the dry today.
Picture courtesy of Red House Museum

The original unblended images
(above)

The parade of shops at the Iford Bridge roundabout, seen in 1963 and today (top left and below)

Iford Bridge pictured in March 1957 (left)

An aerial view of the town with the Christchurch Bypass under construction in 1958 (opposite).
Picture courtesy of Kitchenham Ltd

The view along the High Street
from Church Street in the 1950s,
and today
*Early picture courtesy of
Red House Museum*

Bathers enjoying the sunshine at Mudeford Beach in 1973 (left) and in 2014 (top right)

A view of its controversial satellite tracking station (above)

POUND LANE

Looking down Pound Lane from outside 2 High Street around 1950, with the old town pound on the left
Picture courtesy of Red House Museum

The same scene today (inset)

Highcliffe Castle, mainly built from 1831-36, suffered a severe fire in 1967 (far left). As of 1988, the castle's future was still uncertain (left), but today it has been extensively restored with the help of National Lottery cash (below)

BOURNEMOUTH

An inn and a captain's house, the beginnings of the south coast's major holiday resort

The centre of Bournemouth today would be unrecognisable to Lewis Tregonwell, the retired army officer who founded the modern town in 1810.

When Captain Tregonwell arrived, he found only a brook meeting a road at the head of an unspoilt valley. A short distance away was an inn which had recently been built near what is now the Square. Tregonwell bought several acres of land and built a home, which is today part of the Royal Exeter Hotel. He also planted the first of the town's famous pines.

By late Victorian times, the town was booming, with immaculately tended gardens, a pier (the town was already on its second by 1880), and the ornate Mont Dore Hotel,

which is today the Town Hall. The town acquired a prom, some magnificent churches (notably St Peter's, St Stephen's and the Sacred Heart), the Royal Bath Hotel and Sir Merton Russell-Cotes's home, East Cliff Hall – which is today the Russell-Cotes Art Gallery and Museum.

In the 20th century, a host of dazzling Art Deco buildings sprung up, the Daily Echo prominent among them. The Square became the central point for tram services, then trolleybuses, before becoming a traffic roundabout and finally a pedestrianised area.

Entertainment venues came (the Westover Road cinemas, the Pavilion, the BIC) and sometimes went (the Winter Gardens, the

Westover Ice Rink, the IMAX cinema).

Meanwhile, the communities that had once been villages became suburbs of what was now a sprawling town, which for all its changes, remains one of the UK's favourite destinations.

From busy traffic hub to pedestrianisation, The Square seen from Old Christchurch Road in 1955 and today

The Metropole Hotel on May 23,
1943 in the wake of a devastating
bombing raid by the Luftwaffe,
which also wrecked the Central
Hotel in Richmond Hill.
Today, shops and a pub occupy the
site on Holdenhurst Road, near a
memorial plaque unveiled in 1943

Royal London House under construction in 1957, and today, opposite The College's impressive clock tower (main image)

The grand Metropole Hotel in its heyday in 1895, two years after it was built (top left)

The Metropole's replacement, Royal London House, home to offices and a KFC, today (top right)

The changing face of Lansdowne seen from the top of the Roundhouse Hotel.
A large and complicated junction in 1950 (left), with substantial works under way and the Metropole Hotel still a ruin seven years after the tragic bombing, and a busy roundabout with hotels and expanding educational facilities in 2014 (above)

The Square in 1955 with a
trolleybus heading past, and today,
complete with palm trees
1955 image courtesy of
The Francis Frith Collection

Bournemouth trolleybuses outside the Pier Approach swimming baths on their last journey through the town in 1969 (left)

The Pier Approach flyover under construction in May 1972 (top left)

The same scene today (top right)

The approach to Bournemouth's Pier in 1934, showing Sydenham's Library and reading rooms, post office and 'fancy bazaar' (left)
Picture courtesy of The Peters Collection

The Waterfront building, containing the Imax cinema, which stood on the site from 1998-2013 (top left)

The site today, turned into an outdoor performance area (above)

The Pier Approach and West Cliff
in 1918 and today
*Early image courtesy of
The Francis Frith Collection*

Holdenhurst Road from the St. Paul's Roundabout area, looking east towards the railway station on the left and East Cliff Church on the right. Seen here in 1970 and 2014

1970 image courtesy of Kitchenham Ltd

The Pavilion, Bournemouth's theatre and ballroom dating from the 1920s, pictured in 1950 and today

The top of Richmond Hill in 1967, before the roundabout and its trees were removed to make way for the Wessex Way interchange, and the same scene today, with tall office buildings dominating the area

The Daily Echo's art deco building, opened in 1934, still stands on the hill today, where a milkman is pictured making deliveries circa 1890 (left)
1890 picture courtesy of
The Peters Collection

A line of trolleybuses head down Richmond Hill to the Square for the last time in 1969 (right) and the same scene today, with the road now a cul-de-sac (below)

The Square as a busy traffic thoroughfare in 1935, with Bobby's department store in the background

The scene today, Debenhams replaced Bobby's in 1972 (above)

Bournemouth Square circa 1900, with a branch of the small retail chain Leverett and Frye that stood there from 1872-1913. It was replaced in 1915 by the building which now houses Debenhams. Notice the church spire in the earlier image, no longer present today

Bournemouth Square as it looked in 1899, with the town expanding rapidly (left)
Picture courtesy of the Peters Collection

The Square in the 1920s, with the clock donated by Captain HB Norton standing on top of the tram shelter (below)

Bournemouth Square in the 1950s, and today, with a tower bearing the clock that had originally stood atop a tram shelter and, beyond, today's tethered balloon can be seen in the Lower Gardens (right)

A crowd waits at the approach to Bournemouth West railway station in Queens Road in the 1950s (below) and the same scene today (top left)

The station pictured around 1960, before its closure in 1965 (left)

Bournemouth Central railway station, built in 1885 and originally called Bournemouth East, is pictured on a busy day in 1907. The station was renamed Bournemouth in 1967, after the closure of Bournemouth West station, and extensively refurbished in 2000 (opposite)

Children enjoy sailing model
boats in Bournemouth's Pleasure
Gardens around 1900, where
visitors still stop by the Bourne
Stream today
*1900 image courtesy of
the Peters Collection*

POOLE

An ancient sea port and harbour, maritime links have strengthened as the town has changed much over recent decades

Poole had centuries of history behind it before Bournemouth had even got started.

It was already an important town in the 13th century, while Elizabeth I created the office of sheriff, which still exists today.

The town's prosperity was built on overseas trade – and occasionally on smuggling and piracy. Poole still has a number of warehouses from its trading heyday, along with the former homes of wealthy merchants, such as Poole House and West End House.

The town's oldest surviving building is the Town Cellars in Sarum Street, while nearby stands Scaplen's Court, the 15th century building which is now an education centre. The oldest surviving building on the Quay is thought to be the early 17th century Poole Arms.

But much of Poole would be unrecognisable to residents of old. A massive clearance programme from 1959-72 saw more than half the town's pre-1850 buildings demolished. As well as the arrival of tower blocks, the era saw the building of the Arndale Centre, later renamed the Dolphin Centre, and the adjacent bus station. Later in the 1970s, the town acquired the huge Barclays House building and Poole Arts Centre, now called Lighthouse. Poole's power station at Hamworthy was closed in 1988 and later demolished.

Rapid change continued into the 21st century. The old Poole Pottery building on the Quay was replaced by Dolphin Quays. The RNLI – which moved to the town in 1974 – built a new College. And in 2012, Poole's Twin Sails Bridge was opened amid much razzamatazz – a reminder of how much the town owes to the sea.

The construction of Barclays House in 1973 and as seen in 2014 from the roof of the Dolphin Centre

Trade ships moored at Poole Quay around 1900 viewed from the Hamworthy side, with today's scene, including the world-renowned Sunseeker boatyard, on the opposite side (main image)

The original, unblended, pictures (above)

Poole High Street seen in 1910 and today (left)

The scene circa 1910 shows the original railway crossing date (installed in 1872), with the old Electric Theatre on the extreme left (right)

Today, the high street is pedestrianised, while the plaza has given way to Falkland Square (top right)

The view down Poole High Street from Poole Plaza in 1982, with the roads still open to traffic (bottom)

Seen from the High Street, the second phase of Poole Arndale Centre being constructed in February 1980 and The Dolphin Centre in 2014 (left) and the full original images (above)

Poole's Victorian railway station pictured in 1968 (left). The buildings were demolished and initially replaced by prefabricated structures in the 1970s

The current station building, which replaced the prefab station in the late 1980s (above)

Poole's railway station as it looked
in December 1968, with a level
crossing beyond the platforms (left)

The scene today, with the Towngate
flyover where the crossing once
stood (above)

Poole Arts Centre under
construction opposite the bus
station in July 1976 (top)

The centre re-opened after a major
refurbishment in 2002 and became
Lighthouse, Poole's Centre for the
Arts (above)

The blended image on the left
shows how it has transformed the
street scene

Poole bus station pictured in 1970, with construction still going on at the Arndale Centre behind, and as seen today (below)

Bird's eye view taken from
Barclay's House, in 1977, of Poole
Town Centre, and today (inset)

Development work going on in Kingland Road, opposite Poole Arts Centre, in September 1988

The site is today a car and coach park, with the Seldown eco-village seen beyond (right)

KINGLAND R·D·

Kingland Road in Poole with the
Arndale Centre under construction
circa 1967 (below)

The site has changed almost
beyond recognition today (right)

The Arndale Centre and the George roundabout being built in 1970 (opposite)

The same scene viewed from High Street North, today (opposite inset)

View from 1962 of the roundabout where Poole High Street divided, one road leading to Bournemouth and the other to the west (below)

The scene was transformed by the building of the Arndale Centre and the George roundabout, seen in 2014 (right)

The demolition of Poole's power station was a major spectator event when its chimneys came down in 1993

The same scene viewed from flats in Sterte Avenue shows the Hamworthy site, with the approach to the Twin Sails Bridge on the left of the picture (inset left)

The Poole Pottery factory on Poole
Quay pictured in 1977

The building was replaced in
the 1990s by the Dolphin Quays
development of apartments and
shops (top right)

Waves lash Poole Quay at high water, in 1974, and the Quay today with the Thistle Poole hotel (main image)

The Thistle Poole was built on the site of the former gas works, pictured in 1977 (above)

EAST DORSET

From Roman rings, through King Alfred's church to an Art Deco theatre, a charming rural gem

Archaeologists tell us that the first residents of Wimborne may have been there as early as 300BC. The Romans established the Iron Age hill fort of Badbury Rings around 43AD, but it was in King Alfred's time that the town began to assume real importance.

The magnificent Minster – or more properly, the Minster Church of St Cuthburga – was founded around 705AD and was the burial place of King Ethelred, brother of Alfred. Visitors to the town today can still see many wonderful historic buildings. The Priest's House was among its earliest homes, dating from 1600, and has been the town's museum since 1962. Oddfellows Hall was built by the town's Friendly Society in the

mid-18th century, while Deans Court, behind the Minster, has been owned by the Hanham family for centuries. Allendale House was the home of William Castleman, who was instrumental in bringing the railways to the town.

Among the more recent architectural gems are the Tivoli Theatre, built in Art Deco style in 1936. It closed in 1979, only for a community restoration effort to see it successfully re-opened 14 years later.

While the centre of Wimborne retains an old-fashioned charm, the district of East Dorset around it has grown rapidly in recent decades. Villages such as Verwood, Ferndown, West Moors and Corfe Mullen saw their populations

increase dramatically from the 1970s onwards.

But for all the changes, East Dorset remains a superb place to live and visit – as shown by regular studies reporting that its population is among the happiest and longest-lived in the country.

East Street in Wimborne, pictured in 1966 and today

The Square in Cranborne pictured in the 1950s and today

The 12th century Knowlton
Church, under scaffolding in 1961,
and as it is today (left and above)

The Longham bridge, in January
1962 and much busier in 2014

Wimborne Cricket Ground with a
match in progress in 1980
Picture courtesy of Kitchenham Ltd

The Waitrose store on the site today
(inset)

Wimborne railway station pictured in 1963 and the market site which stands there today (top right)

Wimborne Square, in 1971
and today
*Early image coutesy of
Kitchenham Ltd*

NORTH DORSET

St Edward the Martyr, Hovis hill, Georgian gems, one of landscape painting's greats and gorgeous countryside

North Dorset is home to some of the most gorgeous countryside – and some of the most historic buildings – you could hope to find. In the 14th century, Shaftesbury was Dorset's most populous town. It had been attracting pilgrims since King Edward was buried there in 979 after his murder at Corfe Castle and was canonised as St Edward the Martyr.

King Canute journeyed there to pray over the saint in 1038 but had a heart attack there and died. Shaftesbury's fortunes declined when Henry VIII dissolved the monasteries in 1539 and its abbey was demolished. In modern times, its Gold Hill achieved widespread fame as a Northern mill town in the Hovis TV adverts.

Blandford Forum is one of England's Georgian treasures, thanks to the Bastard brothers, John and William, who rebuilt it after fire destroyed three-quarters of the town in 1731.

Some buildings from before the fire remain, including the Old House and the Ryves Almhouses. The most impressive buildings from after the fire include the Town Hall, Corn Exchange, the Church of St Peter and St Paul and the Red Lion, which was once the Bastard's home.

Sturminster Newton was once the home of Thomas Hardy and the dialect poet William Barnes. King Alfred lived there and bequeathed it to his youngest son, Ethelwad and the town is home to a ruined

castle, whose earthworks date from the Iron Age.

Gillingham was where the forces of King Edmund Ironside saw off the Danish invader Canute in 1016, only for Edmund to be assassinated months later. John Constable stayed in the town in 1820 and 1823 and painted several scenes there – one of many people to fall for North Dorset's charms.

Gold Hill at Shaftesbury, pictured circa 1900 and today. *Early image courtesy of Gold Hill Museum*

Salisbury Street in Blandford, pictured in the early part of the 20th century and today (left)

A new pedestrian crossing unveiled in Shaftesbury in July 1953, and the scene today (top rght and above)

Blandford railway bridge pictured in 1978 and the same spot today (top left and right)

Blandford's railway arches being blown up in 1978 (main image)

Tarrant Keynston's post office circa 1920 with the Wimborne Road crossroads beyond, in 2014
Picture courtesy of the S. Jardine Collection

The True Lovers Knot on the Wimborne Road (inset)

Children look curiously at the photographer in East Street, Blandford in 1890 while shoppers and traffic pass by today
Picture courtesy of the S. Jardine Collection

Shaftesbury's Gold Hill, scene of
the famous Hovis advertisement,
pictured around the beginning of
the last century, and today
*1900 picture courtesy of
Gold Hill Museum*

PURBECK

Steam engines, Thomas Hardy's 'Knollsea', a romantic ruin with a murderous history and a World Heritage coastline

The Isle of Purbeck may not really be an island at all, yet it does seem set apart from the everyday world. Where else could you watch a film in a gas-lit cinema and visit a town that has successfully brought back the steam train?

The beauty of the Purbeck Hills and the spectacular vista of what we now know as the Jurassic Coast have been drawing people to the area for centuries.

Swanage was originally a fishing village, first mentioned in an Anglo-Saxon chronicle of 877AD. Its railway turned it into a thriving Victorian resort, immortalised by Thomas Hardy as 'Knollsea', where anyone who was not a boatman was a quarryman.

As well as Victorian attractions such as its pier and Gothic clock tower, the town is home to much more recent buildings such as the Mowlem Theatre, named after successful local builder and former quarry boy John Mowlem. The town's rail link was closed in 1972, but dedicated volunteers saw it re-opened as a steam line.

Wareham, on the banks of the Frome and traditionally the gateway to the Isle of Purbeck, can trace its history to Roman times. It is home to Dorset's only Saxon church, St Martin's, and has magnificent Saxon earthen walls. Much of the town was rebuilt in Georgian times following a devastating fire in 1762. But one of its favourite buildings dates from the 1930s– the gas-lit Rex cinema.

Between Wareham and Swanage stands Corfe Castle, the 11th century fortification which shares its name with the village below – and which still provides the perfect vantage point for taking in the astonishing natural beauty of the area around it.

The seafront at Swanage in 1903, when the 'new' town was still being built, and today

A holiday traffic queue on Wareham's South Street in August 1955 (below)

The same scene on a surprisingly quiet day, in 2014 (left)

North Street, Wareham, in 1910 with the National Provincial Bank prominent, and in 2014 (inset)
Main image courtesy of Wareham Town Museum

The Cross and West Street in
Wareham, seen around 1900
and with modern traffic in 2014
*Early image courtesy of
Wareham Town Museum*

101

Lulworth Castle during the devastating fire of August 29, 1929 (top right)

The castle under restoration in September 1991 (left)

The restored castle as it stands today (above)

Wareham Quay circa 1900, showing
the Church of Lady St Mary, with a
water bowser at the quayside (right)
Picture courtesy of
Wareham Town Museum

Today, the same spot is popular
with tourists (below)

A 1940s paddle steamer, 'moored' in the modern-day Lulworth Cove. The vessel was one of three that brought tourists from Bournemouth and Weymouth on holiday (left)

The cove is also pictured in the 1940s (right) and today (below)

DORCHESTER

An Iron Age village, a significant Roman town, the start of the union movement and a prince's vision

Dorchester is Dorset's oldest town and is packed with fascinating historical sites dating back to Roman and Saxon times, from Iron Age dwellings at the brooding Maiden Castle and Poundbury, to the Roman amphitheatre at Maumbury Rings and the mosaic-floored Roman Town House.

A visit to the Old Crown Court and cells is a fascinating experience, encompassing four centuries of crime and punishment. This is a place most famous for the trial of the six Tolpuddle Martyrs in 1834, who were sentenced and eventually transported to Australia. The court remains almost as it was then.

The town is still very much the 'Casterbridge' of Thomas Hardy's novels. His home, Max Gate, is owned by the National Trust as is his birthplace, Hardy's Cottage, in nearby Lower Bockhampton.

The award-winning Dorset County Museum, founded in 1846, houses a wealth of collections from Dorset life, whether archaeology, geology, natural or social history.

However, the face of Dorchester is changing. Plans remain in place for Poundbury – the Prince of Wales's favourite 'new town' – to become a high-density urban quarter that gives priority to the people. Despite construction only being at the halfway stage, the area has already contributed millions of pounds in demand for goods and services to the local economy.

The development of Brewery Square has added a vibrant new quarter in the heart of the town. The sympathetic approach taken to develop the old Eldridge Pope brewery buildings has given the area a new lease of life through the construction of shops, restaurants, flats and a cinema.

Both developments represent an exciting new chapter in the town's future, with many pages still to be written.

Cornhill in Dorchester, as shown in a postcard from 1908 and as a busy pedestrian thoroughfare today

PEDESTRIAN
ZONE

No vehicles

Except for
loading
4.30 pm - 9.30 am

At any
time

PEDESTRIAN
ZONE

No vehic

Excep
load
4.30

LLOYDS BANK

SOUTH ST.
(CORNHILL)

SHOP
TO LET

Legat Owen
01244 408200
www.legatowen.co.uk

A view along South Street,
Dorchester, from the entrance to
North Square in 1908 and today

A view down a century in High East Street, Dorchester, with the King's Arms on the left, circa 1911, and the busy scene today

Crossing Cottage No. 43 was a local landmark at the entrance to Dorchester South station for many years (below)

Today, an Odeon cinema dominates the scene (right)

Fordington Hill in the early 20th century. Fordington was originally a village separate from Dorchester

Today, the area is an attractive suburb of the town (inset)

WEYMOUTH

Two feuding ports, a Royal charter, a sweeping Georgian masterpiece and the home of an architectural giant

Weymouth's harbour has always been a hub of activity, whether serving as a major port in times gone by or more for pleasure as it is now, alongside its fishing industry. The harbour has two main parts as well as the ferry terminal. Custom House Quay is on what was the Melcombe Regis side and the Old Harbour is on the Weymouth side. The two harbours didn't always exist in harmony, they were often opposed over trading rights, until the two were eventually united by Royal Charter of Elizabeth I. The Borough of Weymouth and Melcombe Regis came into being in 1571. Harmony was not immediate however, it was to be several years before the act of unity became a reality in practice.

A bridge linking the ports of Weymouth and Melcombe Regis was first built in 1597, with various replacements built since then, the most recent opened in 1930. Weymouth was also home to the architect Sir Christopher Wren who was the Member of Parliament for Weymouth in 1702, and controlled nearby Portland's quarries from 1675 to 1717.

Perhaps the most iconic architecture in Weymouth is the Georgian Esplanade.

The seafront is composed of Georgian terraces, now converted into apartments, shops, hotels and guest houses. The buildings were constructed in the Georgian and Regency periods, between 1770 and 1855, by architects such as

James Hamilton, commissioned by wealthy businessmen, including those that were involved in the growth of Bath.

Weymouth was bombed by the Luftwaffe in the Second World War and, as with so many towns around the country, some of the destroyed historic buildings were replaced with less than pleasing edifices.

Weymouth's seafront and grand Royal Terrace circa 1910, with visitors arriving by horse-drawn carriage, and today

Weymouth's promenade and Brunswick Terrace, from an Edwardian postcard, and as seen today (left)

The original early image showing a bandstand, now gone (below)

Weymouth Esplanade, looking towards the King's Statue – erected in 1872 in tribute to George III – in times gone by and in 2014

A busy working Weymouth Harbour in 1924, and the same scene today (main image)

The two unblended images (above)

This idyllic scene at the village pond in Sutton Poyntz, near Preston, remains unspoiled today

Rodwell Road at Boot Hill, Weymouth, in times gone by and today. The homes on the left are the 'Edwards Houses', built by former Weymouth MP Sir Henry Edwards in the late 19th century.

Custom House Quay in Weymouth during one of the floods which hit the area periodically

The town is better protected today (right)

Weymouth Harbour in the days when the town offered a typewriting office and twice-nightly film showings at the Palladium

The bar Rendezvous occupies the Palladium's building today (right)

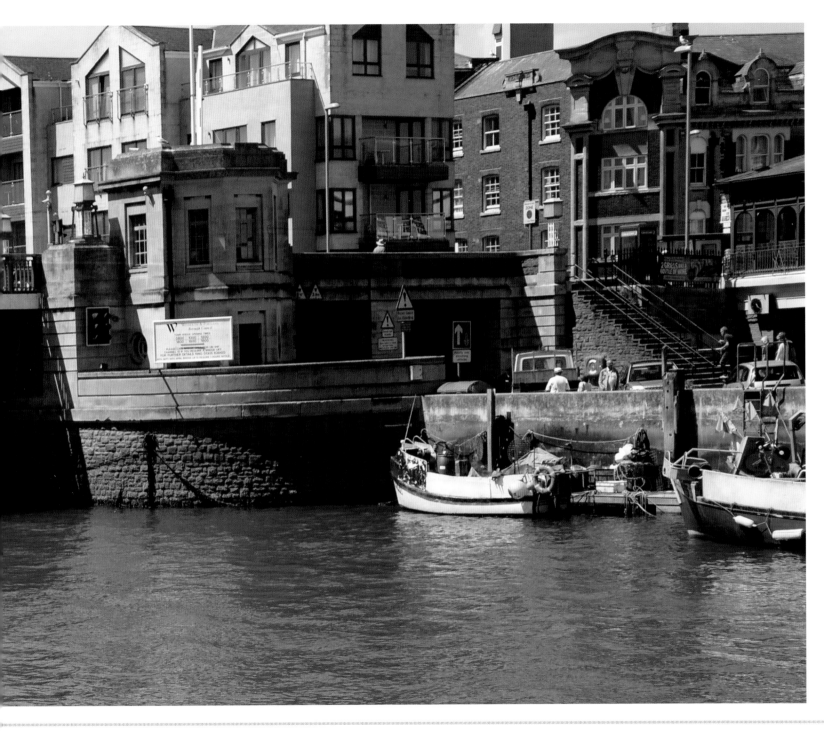

Weymouth Harbour's lifting bridge has linked the two halves of the town since 1830. This blend of pictures shows how warehouse buildings have become waterfront homes (left)

The chimney standing in the background of this view of Sutton Poyntz, circa 1920s, may have belonged to the Weymouth Waterworks Company pumping station (left). It is absent from the scene today (above)
Early picture courtesy of the Andy Hutchings Collection

Radipole Lane in Weymouth, showing Radipole Lake, in 1910 (right) and the same scene today (below)

Cottages at Sutton Poyntz in the 1960s and the village scene today (inset)
Picture by Frederick Masters

This view across Weymouth Harbour from Nothe Parade shows Weymouth Pavilion as it was originally (left)

The building was wrecked by fire in 1954 and replaced with the current structure (above)

This view of Cove Row shows the harbourside as it was between Cove Street and Hope Street (bottom left)

Many of the original buildings are absent from the scene today (below)

This view of Weymouth's Royal Terrace and King's Statue shows a notice advertising the town's regatta

George III still looks down on the terrace today (right)

PORTLAND

The building blocks of international icons, a military massacre, smugglers, pirates and the Olympic fleet

The island of Portland has an individual character which has been shaped over the years by its fiercely independent residents.... and the stone beneath their feet. Maintaining its liberty in Dorset until the 19th century, this ancient Royal Manor has a rich and illustrious history.

Jutting out into the English Channel for four and a half miles, it has three lighthouses - the most famous of which is the much-photographed Portland Bill.

Dr Marie Stopes was the owner of the 18th century Old Higher Lighthouse, and the birth control pioneer founded Portland's museum in 1930.

The island has hosted invaders, pirates, convicts and artists.

But it is Portland Stone which has shaped the buildings of the island and cities far beyond.

Portland Stone has been quarried since Roman times and was quickly established as London's choice of building stone. It was used to build St Paul's Cathedral, the National Gallery and New Scotland Yard.

In 1803 Portland was the scene of the Easton Massacre, in which the British armed forces shot dead three people while attempting to press men into service.

One resident, Mary Wray, was wounded when a crowd attempted to rescue a man from the press gang. She later died from her injuries.

Church Ope Cove, on the eastern side of the island, was a famous smuggling beach and pirates' graves can still be seen there today.

In 1797, John Penn, grandson of the founder of Pennsylvania USA, visited the cove and was so enchanted he had Pennsylvania Castle built for him nearby.

Portland recently played host to the sailing events of London 2012 and still attracts visitors who love to explore its enigmatic charms.

The Straits at Portland, seen in a postcard from circa 1925, and today

Portland's Old Higher Lighthouse circa 1895, when it was still working in tandem with the Old Lower Lighthouse to protect the area's shipping
Picture courtesy of the Stuart Morris Collection

The lighthouse has been disused since 1906 but remains open to visitors, while the buildings around it are used as holiday lets (top right)

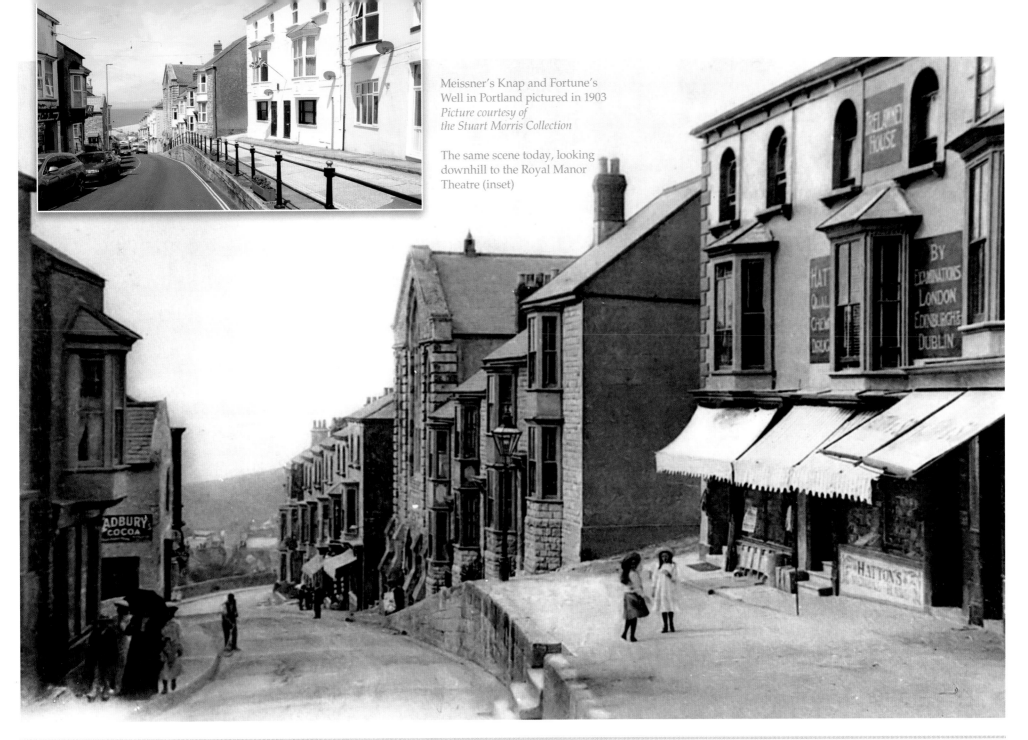

Meissner's Knap and Fortune's Well in Portland pictured in 1903
Picture courtesy of the Stuart Morris Collection

The same scene today, looking downhill to the Royal Manor Theatre (inset)

Victoria Gardens on Portland, as they looked in 1924 and the same scene today (main image)
Early image courtesy of the Andy Hutchings Collection

Portland's Easton Gardens, circa 1900, with its Clock Tower and the bandstand which hosted weekly concerts (top right)
Picture courtesy of the Andy Hutchings Collection

The bandstand disappeared in 1966, but the Clock Tower is a listed building (above right)

Victoria Square, Portland, in 1976, with Chesil Beach Motors selling the new Ford Cortina
Picture courtesy of the Stuart Morris Collection

The company relocated after flooding and the block was demolished, as can be seen from the new picture (inset)

Chiswell, the oldest settlement on Portland, developed as a fishing village around Chesil Cove. Many of its stone buildings (above) remain preserved today (inset)

Castletown on Portland, seen circa 1895 and as it is today (main image)
Early image courtesy of the Stuart Morris Collection

Easton Lane as it was in the days of the horse-drawn carriage and the village pump (top) and as the busy route through Portland that it is today (above)
Picture courtesy of the Andy Hutchings Collection

Victoria Square on Portland, designed in the 1860s to coincide with the arrival of the railways
Picture courtesy of the Stuart Morris Collection

The railway closed to passengers in 1952, the Terminus Hotel becoming the Little Ship 20 years later (inset)

Portland's 19th century Avalanche Church as it looked in times gone by
Picture courtesy of the Stuart Morris Collection

The church is partially obscured by trees in the modern view from the nearby road junction (inset)

These cottages at Brandy Row, Chiswell, are typical of the kind that could be found in every Portland village (left) Countless cottages were demolished rather than modernised (top left) and the area today looks very different (top right)
Early images courtesy of the Stuart Morris Collection

Fortuneswell on Portland at the junction with High Street, around 1895 (main image) and today (bottom right opposite)
Picture courtesy of the Stuart Morris Collection

WEST DORSET

One of the country's most beautiful areas, a sweeping World Heritage coastline, historic buildings and the seat of rebellion

The towns and villages of West Dorset have been largely shaped by the sweeping coastline and rolling countryside that make it one of the most beautiful parts of the country. Much of the region is designated as an area of outstanding natural beauty. It has inspired poets, authors, film directors and TV personalities from Henry Fielding and John Fowles to Hugh Fearnley-Whittingstall.

The West Dorset coast is famous for its rocks and fossils dating back to the Jurassic period 190 million years ago, and now has World Heritage Site status.

Bridport and its neighbouring resort West Bay are vibrant towns with a fascinating history. Bridport's origins date back at least to Athelstan's time in the 10th century, and merit mention in the Domesday records of 1086.

Just south is the busy harbour village of West Bay, with working fishing boats, pubs and restaurants. To the west, on the A35 is the village of Morecombelake, home of Moores Dorset Biscuits, including the famous Dorset Knob, the bakery has been in use since 1880.

Also in the immediate area are Mapperton House, Mangerton Mill and Broadwindsor Craft and Design Centre.

Lyme Regis is a fascinating seaside town with a tangle of narrow streets and shops tumbling down to the harbour with its famous Cobb, a massive curved stone wall.

In 1685 the Duke of Monmouth landed at the Cobb and declared himself king during his ill-fated attempt to remove James II.

Beaminster, an attractive small town in the Vale of the River Brit, has an historic centre featuring more than 200 listed buildings. There are beautiful walks along Dorset's 'hidden valley' with rare flowers, badger setts and old water mills.

A vintage postcard of West Bay harbour and the same scene, with modern yachts and pleasure craft today

East Street in Bridport around Edwardian times, with the William Elmes drapers and outfitters dominating the street scene (above) and this scene blended with today's modern shopping high street (main image)

An Edwardian view of Red Lane, Abbotsbury, where a cottager has been harvesting the Knolls withy beds above nearby Ferny Hole; and Red Lane as it is today

Bridport celebrates Coronation Day, June 22, 1911 (opposite main image)
Picture courtesy of the Keith Alner Collection

A modern view of the same scene, looking up Victoria Grove (top right)

The picturesque valley village of Powerstock in West Dorset, seen in a vintage postcard and today (left)
Early image courtesy of the Keith Alner Collection

The beautiful Bride Valley village of Burton Bradstock, seen in a vintage postcard (top right)
Picture courtesy of the Keith Alner Collection

Today, the post office and shop occupies the same spot, but cars have replaced cattle in the street scene (bottom right)

Many of Bridport's buildings date from the 18th century. East Street, shown in bygone times and today, remains a busy thoroughfare (left) *Picture courtesy of the Keith Alner Collection*

West Bay harbour and its Pier Terrace building, designed by Edward Schroeder, in Edwardian times (below). The view today was captured from the harbour's new west pier, known as the Jurassic Pier

Bathing machines were dotted around Lyme Regis beach circa 1900 but have given way to deckchairs and windbreaks today
Picture courtesy of the Lyme Regis Philpot Museum

Families enjoy a visit to Lyme
Beach in 1903
*Picture courtesy of
the Lyme Regis Philpot Museum*

The beach and seafront retain their
charm today (top right)

This 1950s view of West Bay shows the remains of the eroded Battery Point, with a kiosk in the centre

The same scene is shown from West Cliff today (inset right)